Company of Ghosts

Lucy Dixcart

Indigo Dreams Publishing

First Edition: Company of Ghosts
First published in Great Britain in 2024 by:
Indigo Dreams Publishing
24, Forest Houses
Cookworthy Moor
Halwill
Beaworthy
Devon
EX21 5UU

www.indigodreamspublishing.com

ISBN 978-1-912876-83-9

British Library Cataloguing in Publication Data. A CIP record for this book can be obtained from the British Library.

Designed and typeset in Palatino Linotype by Indigo Dreams.
Cover design by Ronnie Goodyer.
Printed and bound in Great Britain by 4edge Ltd.

Papers used by Indigo Dreams are recyclable products made from wood grown in sustainable forests following the guidance of the Forest Stewardship Council.

For Mum

Acknowledgements

Some of the poems in this collection, or versions of them, first appeared in the following publications: *Acumen, Fenland Poetry Journal, Ink Sweat & Tears, Lighthouse, Marble Poetry, SOUTH, Stand, The Rialto, Wild Court.* Some were included in my pamphlet *Faint,* published by Wild Pressed Books in 2020.

Several poems were published by Carcanet in the Brotherton Poetry Prize Anthology II, edited by Simon Armitage. 'Tortoise' was the winner of the 2020 Lord Whisky Sanctuary Poetry Competition. 'Summer Job' was highly commended in the Winchester Poetry Prize 2023, and 'Syzygy' was shortlisted for the 2023 Canterbury Festival Poet of the Year competition.

My thanks to Rebecca Goss and Julia Webb for providing valuable critiques and advice at different stages of the creation of the manuscript. Thanks also to Ronnie Goodyer and Dawn Bauling at Indigo Dreams Publishing for giving *Company of Ghosts* a home.

Previous Publications

Faint, Wild Pressed Books, 2020.

CONTENTS

Company of Ghosts

Pandora

Today, I will harvest the glittering rind of a chocolate bar;
a discarded surgical mask; a sodden shopping list;
a bottle top prised from mud. These are the things
I will put in the box today.

I was given gifts.
I was a gift. I am the giver
of gifts. Gifted.

He wanted perfect. He had a vision.
The sculptor. He drew her. In his mind.
He scraped clay from the earth. He kneaded and scored
and carved with the finest of knives
and he saw that she was good.

Tell me the price of fire.
Tell me I was a beautiful missile.
Tell me you're glad.

It is not a box. It is a jar
and I will never stop filling it
with chip wrappers and panic attacks
and cyber criminals and dirty laundry and disease
and the look you give me that says
still not enough.

Faint

I am feeling hysterical again.
I have dwindled to 18 inches, lungs trussed, bones bowing.
Drifting, I feel the sea monster squeeze
until my hull creaks and cracks; until my innards do-si-do.

Fetch the smelling salts. Take me, swooning,
to my fainting couch and arrange me just so.
Tend me as I loll, insensible and decorative,
awaiting the doctor and his therapeutic manipulations.

Tell me, future sister, where will you go
to loosen your laces, gorge yourself on air?
Where will you go when your womb wanders?
When you drown in the shallows?

There must be space in your day for a fainting spell,
a hallucination or two?

In Concert

At night, my lost sisters rise –
floating ghosts manacled with kelp,
faces moon-soaked, lassoed by their own
salty hair.

Each sings her last moment –
a job declined, a child that wasn't,
a door closed, or opened.
I've shed a self at every threshold.

Years have made me sharp,
but what power we had before –
our blended voices whispering
all possible futures.

Moments played and replayed
like violins – we stood on the top step
knowing we could fly – how am I
still standing? What I want

is to wade into black water,
my dress a perfect bell,
and scoop each me onto my hip:
I love you.   Forgive me.

The Prophecy

In the underworld, she hurls herself daily
from the platform. Once she misses the train
and slithers leg-first into the crevice.
Suited commuters dip their newspapers,
then resume reading. After an age,
a guy with dreadlocks hauls her to safety.

She runs for a coach that will stutter
back down the same road an hour later;
accepts a filthy Lion Bar
from a stranger – safer than declining.

One evening, heading home, she feels lighter.
A man bellows across the highway:
You'll grow old. And your tits'll sag.
And what'll you do then?

Ghost Hunter

Her grown-up self is haunting
this city street – that is the game –
but which face is hers? Suited
people drain into the earth,
already deactivated. She changes
her mind. She can't

lost myself. Rummaging
through cellophaned portraits,
I claimed a dark-haired girl
until a friend said, *What are you doing?*
That isn't you   she's nothing like

reports that my double
was in this café, muttering
to an invisible partner. I'm always
on standby, poised to grab
her sleeve before

cross this border   squeeze
through the coffin hole   unspool

like a tree she has sealed
all her mothers beneath her skin –
they interrupt her constantly
with love and reproach   *you could*
have been

the old woman smiles –
she has waited for me
all this time. Her face
is a gorgeous treasure map.
Today I am brave   we talk and talk.

Isolations

i.
In my hooping phase I learn isolation
is an illusion. Seemingly unhooked
from the compass of your arm,
the hoop turns, but does not travel.

ii.
On the solstice,
I stand barefoot on grass
and spin a slow circle,
casting an invisible line across earth and oceans.

iii.
What sequence of events brought us here,
to this path,
to autumn's soft disintegration,
to this beech leaf's single, spiralling journey?

iv.
Last night we talked for hours.
You were unchanged, mapped by my synapses
in minute detail. When I woke,
the moon was rolling into the treeline,
luminous as an egg.

v.
Every morning,
gulls rise like prayers over scalped fields,
and I fall into my skin for the first time.

I Claim This Sky

All winter I have kept vigil
on these lichen-licked branches,
compacting myself like stone.

I've laid out the bones of my dead,
glued my bloodied edges
back together,

shredded my pages
and fed them to the wind –
a lost language keeps its own secrets.

I open my wings, show my breadth
to the sky. Feathers flash
like teeth.

Now
I am nothing but myself,
an arrow set for blue.

Paper Dolls

She did well,
my secret twin – kept us alive,
deflected blows,

absorbed each wound
into our body, quiet as a tree.
I didn't notice her leave

until the wind whistled in
and a bird
flew from my mouth.

Later
I unfolded myself
like a chain of paper dolls

and found the ledger snipped,
two featureless hands
reaching for air.

Dust

Halfway upstairs
a shaft of sun illuminates
a universe of particles:
my silent twin.

I scatter my own remains,
feather to earth
with every footfall.
Discarded parts minute my routes.

Follow the silver trail
to the first of us:
everything I was
still is.

Event Horizon

At the point of no return,
a cosmic whirlpool
funnels you into forever.

In this quiet containment,
choice is revoked.
Every direction leads to the eye –

a swig of light;
planets tossed back like Maltesers –
it all goes down the same.

Don't look at me like that.
Spaghettification
is more fun than it sounds,

your atoms uncoiling
past the elastic limit
as time opens like a fan.

Ēanswīþ

The builders are thirsty –
I strike the earth with my staff
and tremors sing down to the holy spring.

Water shoulders through clay,
heaves itself uphill
and plunges into the pond.

This princess can do it all –
peel clouds from your eyes; stir new growth
in the beam carpenters cut too short.

Go ahead – eat the stolen goose.
Then give me an hour to rebuild its skeleton
and coach it back to flight.

You can keep your prince.
I've got too much to do
engineering the world and fixing mistakes.

But some things can't be mended.
Young as the sky, I recline in my lead casket,
fold myself into the wall.

Centuries rustle past.
Then workmen grope through splinters
and fish for treasure – a crystal rib, a shining tooth.

BBC, 6th March 2020:
"Human remains found hidden inside the wall of a Kent church are thought
to be those of one of the earliest English saints."

Bronze Age Boat

Dover Museum

Ancient oak, stitched with yew,
sealed with beeswax and plugged with moss.
Aboard its planks, voyagers launched –
curious, hungry – into the waves.

Waterlogged and packed with silt,
the earth devoured the vessel whole.
Millennia passed; buildings grew.
Then a skylight opened above.

Hauled from the underworld it rose,
deftly split; quickly submerged.
Recombined, it sits behind glass,
dimly lit, holding its breath.

Princess Alexandra and the Glass Piano

I was a child when I swallowed the piano.
My jaw unhinged and down it slid: keys, strings, pins.
A dream, I imagined, until a crunch punctuated my footsteps
and hammers chinked holes in my thoughts.

Rules to live by when glass underlays your skin:
glide like moonlight, your movements unperceived.
Then halve your speed. Position each foot with care.
Wrap yourself in air. Shun stairs.

If interior music sounds, stand still for hours,
taking very small breaths.

Each night, catastrophic variations unfold.
A wrinkled rug. A fall. A name, abruptly called.
Fracture: cacophony: shatter, crash, chime:
a hailstorm of splinters: my bloody demise.

No marriage for me. My ivory is not for playing.
Swathed in white, I snail the floor –
a wrapper for shrapnel; an unwritten score.

*Born in 1826, Princess Alexandra of Bavaria was a German princess who
believed she had swallowed a glass piano.*

Injuries

i.
Volcano palmed,
red floods from the fleshy crater.
Look, says the teacher,
look what she's done.
This is why you should be careful with scissors.

ii.
Sizzling rack of lamb, ribs buttressed.
Shouldering the door topples the structure,
but the man in the kitchen –
Feet stumble forward. Flesh brands flesh. Eyes flood grey.
I proffer the plate, unpeel my wrist. It burns all night.

iii.
Weever fish, I later learn, skulk below sand,
thrusting a spiked sail when soles descend.
I sag on shingle, punctured, poisoned.
Cliff steps stretch skyward.
No one notices.

In the Panelled Room

My body is a library,
my worth measured in Greek symbols.
Sash windows admit only shadows.

House plants sag, starved of sunlight –
something quieter is blooming
behind oak.

Like everyone here,
I don't play well with others –
we're all teeth.

I pin notes to my door,
find them gone. Days thin to strings –
if I pulled an end, I would run

and run. Silver lights flicker.
The shadows wear faces.
A blackbird

sings at midnight
as blue clots on the page.
What it means, I can't say.

Summer Job

Salt-stung,
I tossed the wreckage of my life
into the ferry's wake, and now this island
has always been home.

I hand out meals in a gingham dress
and sleep above the bar, ears firmly plugged.
In the fridge, trayfuls of crabs
sign slowly with boxing glove claws.
When I reach for the cheesecake,
I swallow a scream.

I've kissed an unkempt stranger
and swum round the headland,
chased by skinless monsters.
I've stumbled through sea fog
at the monument to drowned sailors;
seen stars drip from a cave's vaulted roof.

I've danced to Britney and swerved my eyes
from men pissing behind the bins.
In the ruined house, a workman
told me secrets. At night I dream
of future children.

This conjured world gleams like fool's gold.
Beyond the moat, shadows and heartache
and September are mobilising.
I fill my eyes with glitter.

Work Experience

Mushrooms thrive in chicken manure,
but there's a rumour the farm is dabbling
with faeces from the local zoo.

We traipse into the shed: a corrugated half-cylinder.
I wrangle a ladder that's taller than me,
cram blue punnets onto a metal tray.

Armed with my curved blade, I ascend.
White froth swells imperceptibly into umbrellas.
For £2.12 an hour, I sever stalk after stalk.

Some are beaded with red.
Some membranes leak rancid fluids.
The mites get everywhere.

We dunk our knives in chemicals (*hello
dermatitis*), then decamp to the staff room,
turn tea-splashed pages. Smoke coils and weaves.

One day, the maintenance guy is maimed
as he cleans a machine that crushes things. Another day
we shuffle outside, avert our eyes from the eclipse.

*

Over Christmas I work two jobs:
an early shift at the sorting office;
a late shift at a restaurant.

In my daybreak life I become an expert
on London postcodes. At night I learn
to balance things on my wrists – *three plates, or you're fired*.

Mornings are predictable – *tea o'clock*, the men shout
every hour. We're told to scribble out unfranked stamps –
I doodle robins and holly.

The evenings, though. We're banned
from writing down orders – *just remember what they said!*
Worst of all, dessert is announced by a pageant of girls

showing off platters with hastily learnt descriptions.
One night, I have to offer *spotted dick and custard*
to a hundred tipsy diners.

*

Striding through the carpet-tiled office
come the curators of romance.
Their rules are exacting. Indecisive men?
Think again. Our hero is ruthless, loaded –

a billionaire boss or a Greek tycoon.
The heroine may have sworn off love,
but by chapter ten she'll be all wrapped up:
newlywed, pregnant with twins.

The published authors know the score.
More fertile is the slush pile
where rogue themes frolic –
a gamma hero; a two-timing bride.

As the new recruit, I'm indecently keen,
prising concertinaed pages
from the printer; dispensing caffeine
to my editors – the one with shark eyes;

the one who can't remember my name.
At the station, posters warn of machete attacks.
I haul virgin manuscripts onto the train,
eyes carefully dimmed. Later, I sift for diamonds.

*

The person returning is not
who she was before, even if she's wearing the right clothes
(larger than last time) over damp breast pads,

even if she's forced her feet
into shoes that hurt, even if she's brushed her hair.
So she's not prepared when she steps

warily into a place that was familiar once,
but is now off-kilter, desks misaligned,
books moved, someone else at her computer,

blinking, bemused. *Oh, are you back today?*
Worse are the waxwork people, oblivious
of the shift in reality: unpicked, resewn.

All she can do is reclaim her desk and play her part,
clicking and writing and saying the right sorts of things,
holding on until half past five when she can return.

Wrong Things

i.
Running on hope,
I sing into the silence.
Their faces do not flicker.
As they begin, I know this is the end.

ii.
Defeat is not graceful.
It always goes the same way. The ping pong
of pompous emails. Moonlight crawling over the bed.
Again and again, I lattice words into a new reality,
then drop my hands and watch it all unhook.

iii.
When he asked *Why?*
a spider crept from my ear
and silence set between us like glass.

iv.
Sometimes it's enough to walk away
from the wrong thing. To say, *not this.*

Café at the End of the Pier

Work is a walk over water
– past fishermen, with their flasks and hooks
and weatherproof patience; past benches with flaking paint,
flanked by streetlamps and scratched Perspex windows
– everything in parallel.

To walk over water
is to leave the seafront, where tall buildings glower
in the same direction like a family,
and stride with Roman intention
to a refuge of timber and glass – the ocean's gatehouse.

Once inside, drape the sea across your back,
order black tea, drizzle words onto your screen.
Women with prams will circle you,
scenting the peeled flesh of a fellow mother
– repel them with invisible quills.

Between paragraphs, try to place
the man in the corner who knows Hugh Grant.
Study the girl with fuchsia hair
and plimsolls and twinkling cheeks.
She slumps below her parents' volleys,

twitching her thumb over her phone,
then shoves back her chair,
lit by one of life's rare starbursts.
Her absence lengthens like putty.
Everyone waits, but she never returns.

Motherhood

When the door swings open,
sunlight barges in and Claire follows,
laughing at my bewilderment.
She got the card, is touched I thought of her
after so long. Joy whistles past –

her eyes are sailing;
her face a ledger of wasted gifts,
failed interventions.
Looming behind her
is a boyfriend who reeks of danger

and I think of the baby in his highchair
and I usher them out with promises
of some future meeting –
I am already cancelling the meeting.

Later I follow the buggy over baked mud,
past the miniature pony.
I'm here for the blackberries,
dreaming of jellies and crumbles,
my striped skin the price of fruit –

he is sleeping now, he is perfect.
I settle on bleached grass,
sweep ants from my legs. Part of me
has become bright and terrifying.
Like a tree, I must shed all other details.

What I Missed

I say I'm preserving the season –
simmering handpicked moments
into hot froth until they coagulate;
sealing their colours behind glass –

but I'm getting sloppy. Drafts languish
on dead hard drives. Stories mingle
behind cupboard doors, ready to avalanche.
Diary pages show whole days bleached undone.

I can't save everything. The inches I meant
to pencil on the wall wriggled free –
the boy is sunflower-high now,
his ascent forever unsaid

like the anecdote my grandmother
didn't finish, or the poem that teacher
kept in her folder all those years,
just in case.

Reunion

She's waiting at the porter's lodge
in her flowery jeans.
She tuts as I navigate the quad –
my map is full of holes. I think of the first time.
October winds, dead leaf confetti.

A piano abuts the bed. Her face is snow.
Crushed by clever underwear,
I ease myself into the dress, inch by inch.
Read all about it: python swallows entire cow.
She laughs angrily.

The bar. She's knocking back shots.
Champagne. I remember the song.
Milk-heavy, spinning away, I land in Hall
beside an old foe. He quizzes me
about my job – his is better.

She's rolling her eyes,
propels me to some former friends. We sift
through weddings, children, work – nothing sticks.
I call for help, but she's jigsawed apart
and all her edges are missing.

Drizzle gleams yellow.
I reclaim my room and plumb myself in –
this metronome is my soundtrack.
Voices rise, subside. I leave before dawn,
tugged by an unseen cord.

Birth Day Messages

You can light them now.
A flurry of photos. Blazing jars of wax
brighten sylvan altars and windowsills.
One is heel stone to an amethyst henge.
Another is strapped to the passenger seat
for a candlelit drive down the M25.

She is doing beautifully.
This candle has made me one of many.
It follows me from room to room.

We are filling the pool.
This is a slow burner.
The wick is the stigma of a molten flower.
The flame is a snake's tongue, rapidly tasting the air.

Little one is back-to-back.
A hospital bed. Haggard smiles.
The flame sinks below the rim.
Blowing feels like violence.

I wake to silence, swipe another match.
Dread spews white threads.

We have a beautiful baby girl.
My phone gyrates – a feast of messages.
The flame shimmies,
pours darkness from its shoulders.

At a Birth Blessing, guests may be given candles to take home. Once the expectant mother is in labour, the candles should be lit until the baby is safely delivered.

While You Sleep

A galaxy swirls
within this strand of hair –
electrons orbit,
and between each atom,
unseeable space.

A meshwork of filaments
scaffolds your cells.
Motor proteins haul cargo,
legs flip-flopping
with cartoon panache.

Your blood
could be engaged
in high-tech warfare,
bacteria engulfed
by macrophage assassins –

all your components
have perfect purpose.
Enzymes unwind your last meal.
Chromosomes rattle out
endless self-portraits

while you curve
the soft machinery of your skin
against my back, unaware
of your heartbeat
driving through the night.

Sulis Minerva
The Roman Baths, Bath

Your shuttered eyes smoulder,
mottled bronze bright against black –

goddess of the sacred spring;
agent of punishment.

Curses swirled in your healing waters:
ancient wrongs buffeting votive deposits.

The Gorgon guards your shattered temple.
Magic remains, embalmed.

I loose the child. Hands dip
in your hot currents. Steam peels from green.

We follow paths of worn stone.
Tepidarium, laconicum. The Great Bath.

I have no lead tablet to cast, no enemy to smite.
Filling paper cones

I gulp down your foreign minerals,
inviting miracles.

Fifth

Dusk says *now*
and the children stream downhill,
volleying wild cries;
swinging homemade lanterns.

Neon wands joust
and families scatter into shadows.
Voices soar on the same dial
that dims the day.

Circle the pyre. Conjure a flame.
Scorch your face and breathe in heat.
Watch embers ascend, then parachute
to mudding grass.

Keep hold of your smallest in the dark.
Await the panic of wings
as the first firework
cracks you open.

Forest School in Winter

We coalesce in the car park with others
of our kind, then file into the forest,
stiff-limbed in thermal layers.

Women circle the fire, eyes leaking
as children flambé marshmallows. *Remember
the respect position*, hisses an old timer.

Another mum passes a steaming mug.
Allies for today, we hunch together like hens
then shuffle to the mud kitchen,

crumbling leaves pasted to our wellies.
The girl teeters on logs and feeds things to pigs.
At the queue for the zip wire

she balks, wary of dislodging
a loose tooth. With gloved hands,
I guide the seat through a gentle swoop.

Twelfth Night

Now I reverse my rotations,
cat's cradle the coloured lights,
ease bauble strings
over softening needles.

This ritual is another kind of magic –
stars unhooked,
pins twisted from plaster,
armchairs dragged

back into their footprints.
Pared and replenished
I blink at the featureless dawn,
the annual *what's next?*

January Goals

When this grey dissipates,
I'll skid down a muddy riverbank
in wellies, and spot brown trout
as long as my arm, slinking beneath willow.

Cold-cheeked,
I'll scatter a crowd of dithering coots
and jostle rosehips and crab apples
dangling from witchy fingers.

I'll stand below the angel tree
with its ribbons and trinkets,
and read about the young mother
who shared my first name.

I'll find a new molehill,
sink a foot into its dark crumble,
then crouch to a clutch of green spears,
rising, rising.

Storm

The valley churns and stirs –
white noise, bluescale
of flapping threads,
uncaught endings.

From my bed I listen
to the break and fall of things;
imagine the roof unpicked;
the trampoline tossed against masonry.

Trees clatter.
Fingernails drum on glass.
The giant blows into his shell.

In the morning we emerge
to stillness. Stars glint from branches.
Lichen wands crisscross the drive.
Rainwater tops the pond
like a fresh quilt.

Abbey Gardens, Bury St Edmunds

If I live to be a hundred,
bring me to these gardens
and guide me through the maze of ruins.

Like a flint and mortar column
rising from seed-tipped grass,
I will stand on this spot

and study the severed transept –
its rough porthole
claiming a mouthful of sky.

I'll advance like a bride
through the crypt's carcass,
ankles half-swallowed by green,

past grey rib stubs
and the jawbones of fallen windows.
Pausing by a piece of staircase

I'll curl my feet
to the shape of cobbled treads
and watch children

spiral into air,
my eyes diffused
to countless coordinates.

Concentric

A storm whips back centuries of sediment
with a magician's flair. *Now you see it.*
The seaside strolls of ankylosaurs and therapods
were written in rock all along. Further out,
mammoth tusks stir below haddock and cod.

Nothing here is new. Not the freshest of eggs,
composed like a hymn before the first sky.
Not blossom. Not microchips or morning coffee.
Our cells brim with ancient rainfall. Do you see it now?
The dying pine's carbon was only ever borrowed.

Alumni Picnic

Feet flex on tapered blades,
sampling geometric perfection.

Like the immortal lawn,
a fourteen-year exile
has replaced this ship of Theseus
piece by piece – organs, tissue, skin.

My cargo is memories. My passengers
wear one face; different strains. I am

a copy of a copy
of a copy.

I do not approach the picnicking ghosts
but I have brought my own people.
Together we scrub crayons
over the chapel's printed stone,
prod strawberries with plastic spoons.

The girl's hair starbursts
aboard the space hopper.
The boy laps the garden,
chasing freshly made friends.

Later, exploring,
memories fall like rain.
I catch them, one by one.

Appointment in a Medieval Town

You know my shape, and I know yours,
like the ghosts that hide under every façade –
Lipton's has become a SPAR;
the croissant place now cuts your hair.

Below the top-heavy timber frames,
pigs are called to graze the streets
and boot scrapers yearn for a filthier time.
There's the toll bridge where no-one asks for cash;
the silt-stranded Quay, two miles from the sea.

I left forever, twice, but here I am again –
chiming through the Fisher Gate's flinted arch,
listening for the swish of Thomas Becket's cloak.

Window in the Rock

When you glimpse it
you're crammed into a floating bathtub
with a teenage boy at the tiller,
hurtling towards likely death.

At the moment you think
if I live, Mum can never know,
you look back and spot the rogue pixel
glinting high on the cliff.

You've heard it is not a window
but a void blasted by a long-dead seigneur;
a ledge for winching up vraic;
a hide for spying guillemots.

You don't know your future self
is up there – settling her children,
stepping past DANGER SHEER DROP
into a dark prism that ends in light.

Braced for the rush
she inches forward, palms pressed to rock,
and cheers for a tiny boat 250 feet below
as it vaults the ferry's wake.

Seigneur: feudal lord; the head of state on the Isle of Sark
Vraic: seaweed found in the Channel Islands

Chalk Stream

You rise at Watersend, drink
from white cliffs, draw yourself
endlessly towards the ruined mill,
where coots circle old brickwork
and flag irises drip yellow.

You pass through people like words,
but there is nothing fresher
than your cold kiss on my feet,
or your gifts to the waiting kingfisher –
sliver after sliver of life.

Things I Did Yesterday

Drafted half a white paper before dawn. Performed minor
surgery on the eyebrow of an Easter Bunny that *looked like a sad
mouth*. Baked hot cross buns with lopsided intersections.
Handed out chocolate eggs purchased before lockdown, just in
case. Kept one for myself. Scooped countless buckets of water
from the leaking pond. Uncovered the sticklebacks that
vanished months ago, convulsing in silt. Waded through slurry
and plucked out every snail, every newt, every nymph.
Reached the bottom of the hollow to find it brimming with
minibeasts of unknown denomination. Saved all I could.

Vantage Point

Up here in the gods
everything seems roughly the same.

Toads croak from their ancestral ponds.
A bumblebee drones over heather.
Dog walkers shout pleasantries
from a safe distance.

The sky is scrubbed clean;
the field unexploded yellow.
I gulp down the freshly whipped air,
thankful each piece of this jigsaw still fits.

Distortion comes from other places.
Phones fizz with news of strangers –
symptoms, relapses, tributes.

I await my sister's updates,
google recoveries.

Data Security

Sunrise brings gold
and the crushed sheets in the fireplace
look like they're already ablaze.

I burn old bills, but not the dangerous pages –
poems, diaries, concertinaed letters.
You never know when blackened fragments
will flutter clear, seeding corners
with compromising thoughts.

I should find a way to dispose of them safely.
For now, they're locked in boxes,
barred with alphanumeric passwords,
disguised with fake moustaches,

but too many words have already escaped –
an audit trail that follows me everywhere.

Tortoise

He'll see us all out, my grandfather said. Since then, three generations of children have watched him heave his tessellated shell across the grass – neck elongated; good eye fixed on a dandelion. For decades, he thrived on bread and milk – *totally unnatural,* the website said. He's carb-free now. Solar powered, he rams garden furniture; bulldozes brambles; teeters on edges, clawing at the air with scaled legs. He had a companion in the sixties, but she didn't survive. In the eighties, he devoured a dropped trifle at a garden party. In 2009, he clamped his beak onto a toddler's fingertip, aiming for cucumber. Every spring we await the crackle of hay as he begins his ascent and emerges, unaltered, from his cardboard chrysalis. And year after year we greet him – his custodians, with our changing faces.

Syzygy

The dying things are washed gold –
crisp oregano heads; dull blackberries.

The trees have laced one more corset
around their waists, and somehow

this is the halfway mark:
sepia rooftops, tracing-paper hills;

the scales equalised by before
and after. Let's not pretend

this is balance. Instead, wait for dusk
with its soundtrack – crickets, owls,

a distant motorbike. Feel the night's breath
on your neck. Open your skin to the cold;

count the futures that dried on the branch.
My love, this is where you begin.

Syzygy: the alignment of three celestial bodies, such as the sun, earth and moon during an eclipse.

Indigo Dreams Publishing Ltd
24, Forest Houses
Cookworthy Moor
Halwill
Beaworthy
Devon
EX21 5UU
www.indigodreamspublishing.com